S0-BCL-586

Settlement, Ortschaft
Sight of Interest, Sehenswürd
Mainroad, Hauptstraße
Other Public Road, Landstra
Boundary of Restricted Area
Grenze für militärisches
Schutzgebiet

0   5   10

Kartografi · Erich Zenz · Stockholm

ÖSTERSJÖN

Grynge fiskeläge
Torsburgen
Ardre
Ala
Buttle
Guldrupe
vange
Väte
Mästerby
Eskelhem
Tofta
Kronholmens
golfbana
Utholmen
Pauiken
Västergarn
Sanda
Klinte
Klintehamn
Gannarve
skeppssättning
Fröjel
Djupvik
Lilla Karlsö
Stora Karlsö
Kronvalds
fiskeläge
Kvarnåkershamn
Sproge
Eksta
Levide
Gerum
Fardhem
Linde
Lojsta
Etelhem
Hejde
Lojstahajd
Vallhagar
Slite
Hablingbo
Alva
Hemse
Burs
Rone
Staugard
Eke
Grötlingbo
Havdhem
Näs
Nisseviken
Näs-
udden
Burgs-
viken
Burgsvik
Mölhatte-
träsk
Stor-
sudret
Vamlingbo
Kättelviki
Hoburgen
Sundre
Heligholmen
Raukfält
Holmhällar
Hamra
Faludden
Öja
Fide
Kattlunds gård
Uggårderojr
Ronehamn
Ytterholmen
Grötlingboholme
Horte fiskeläge
När
Lau
Lye
Stånga
Garde
Alskog
Gdrum
Lausbackar
Ljugarn
Raukfält
Folhammar
Austerviken
Närsholmen

Raukfält
Holmhällar

Siv & Key L Nilson

GOTLAND

Pearl of the Baltic
Die Perle der Ostsee

Natur och Kultur

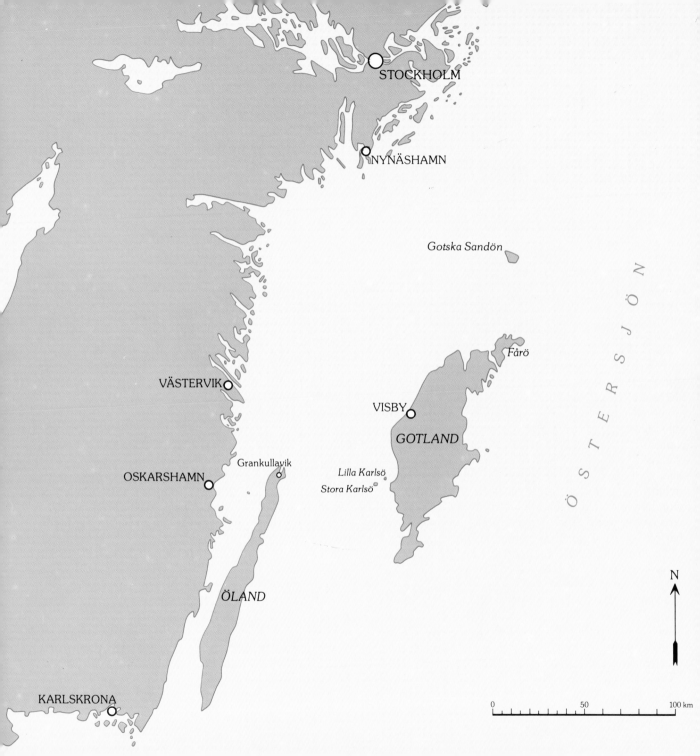

STOCKHOLM

NYNÄSHAMN

Gotska Sandön

Fårö

VISBY

GOTLAND

VÄSTERVIK

Grankullavik

OSKARSHAMN

Lilla Karlsö

Stora Karlsö

ÖLAND

Ö S T E R S J Ö N

N

KARLSKRONA

0   50   100 km

We all of us have our favourite haunts and there are doubtless many who have found their ultimate elysium among the isles of the Baltic. If you have once wandered over the grey limestone marl as winter moves into spring with the sea thundering remorselessly against the shore, if you have witnessed the late summer moors in bloom and heard the distant ringing of lamb-bells at twilight, if you have nibbled wild strawberries while ankle-deep in limpid shoreline water, then you will have succumbed for ever to the most delectable of these islands. Gotland belongs to Sweden, 85 km. from the nearest point on the mainland. The island has not always been Swedish, however. Germans and Danes alike have occupied it and it was not until the middle of the 17th century that it became part of Sweden.

The islanders refer to Gotland itself as "Main island". It is 125 km. in length and 52 km. across at the widest point. Then there is Fårö, the largish island just north of Gotland, Stora and Lilla Karlsö, off the coast southwest of Visby and finally Gotska Sandön, 40 km. north of Fårö.

Many visitors tend to consider the Gotland landscape un-Swedish and there is no denying that parts of the island are reminiscent of more southerly latitudes. In places the limestone bedrock is exposed or, on the barren moorland, covered by the meagrest of soil succouring only the hardiest of flora. Further inland, meanwhile, one comes across verdant glades and arbours; the provenance of most of the wild orchids. There are no less than 35 different species on Gotland. And in addition to these orchids the Gotland islands between them nurture an abundant and unique flora that attracts botanists from all parts of the world. The Gotland fauna, too, differs from that of the mainland. While there are not a great many wild animals, the birdlife abounds and the birdwatcher has many fascinating places to choose between here, especially Stora and Lilla Karlsö.

Gotland is first and foremost farmland, which in itself strongly influences the landscape. Big, handsome farms, billowing grain fields and large vegetable crops. The distance to the mainland, however, is an expensive and complicating factor when selling this produce.

There is considerable fishing around the coasts of Gotland; catches including the finest of salmon, cod and Baltic

Das Leben hat seine paradiesischen Fleckchen, und für den, der einmal die Inseln in der Ostsee aufgesucht hat, besteht kein Zweifel darüber, wo die schönsten zu finden sind. Ist man einmal an dem grauen Kalksteinstrand entlang gewandert, und hat man einmal gesehen, wie sich das Meer ungnädig über alles Lebendige stürzt, hat man im Spätsommer die Heide blühen sehen und in der Dämmerung das eintönige Läuten der Schafglocken gehört, hat man einmal Walderdbeeren schnabuliert, aufgereiht auf einem Grashalm, mit den Füßen in sommerwarmem Wasser baumelnd – ja, dann hat man sein Herz für immer an die beste der Inseln vergeben. Gotland gehört zu Schweden, und die Insel liegt ungefähr 85 km vom schwedischen Festland entfernt. Sie hat allerdings nicht immer zu Schweden gehört. Sowohl Deutsche als auch Dänen haben die Insel beherrscht, erst in der Mitte des 17. Jahrhunderts wurde sie schwedisch.

Gotland wird von den Inselbewohnern "Storön" "Große Insel" genannt. Sie ist etwa 125 km lang und bis 52 km breit. Hinzu kommt Fårö, die große Insel nördlich von Gotland, und die beiden kleinen Inseln Stora und Lilla Karlsö, südwestlich von Visby im Meer gelegen. Auch Gotska Sandö, eine Insel, die sich ca. 40 km nördlich von Fårö befindet, gehört zur Provinz Gotland.

Gotlands Natur wird von vielen Besuchern als unschwedisch aufgefaßt, und sicherlich erinnern bestimmte Teile der Insel an südlichere Breitengrade und an vielen Stellen kommt der Kalkstein zu Tage. Weiter im Inneren von Storön findet man die prachtvollsten "lövsalar" (Laubsäle), die man hier "ängen" nennt. Da gibt es die meisten Orchideen, nicht weniger als 35 verschiedene Arten. Abgesehen von den Orchideen haben die Inseln eine ungewöhnliche und reichhaltige Flora, die Botaniker auf der ganzen Welt intressiert. Auch die Tierwelt auf der Insel unterscheidet sich von der des Festlandes. Es gibt kaum Wild, dafür aber ein außerordentlich reiches Vogelleben. Wer sich für Ornithologie intressiert, für den sind die beiden Karlsöar von besonderem Intresse.

Gotland ist in erster Linie ein Bauernland, man sieht überall große schöne Höfe, wogende Kornfelder und riesige Gemüsepflanzungen. Aber auch der Fischfang ist bedeutend, das Meer ist reich an feinstem Lachs, Dorsch und Strömling.

herring. Another particular delicacy is Gotland lamb. There is more sheep farming on Gotland than anywhere else in Sweden and the flocks which graze on this saline pastureland produce unsurpassable meat. Another contributory factor here may well be the many wild herbs which can add further flavour to the meat.

The early history of Gotland is every bit as significant as life there today. No other place in Sweden has yielded such a wealth of archeological finds. As far as we know the island first became inhabited around 5000 BC. The numerous ship tumuli, i.e. grave fields shaped like a ship's hull, attest that the first Gotlanders were primarily seafarers and as early as the Roman Iron Age Gotland was already a leading Baltic trading centre. Christianity reached the island in the 12th century with its own laws and "ting", i.e. assizes. The "Gutalag", drawn up at about this time, is one of Sweden's oldest provincial law codes.

Despite its imposing early history, the early mediaeval period, especially the 13th century, was nevertheless Gotland's real golden age. It was now that most of the churches were built, mainly beautiful Gothic structures endowed with fine craftsmanship: stone and wooden sculptures, fresco paintings and splendidly worked fixtures and fittings.

It was at this time, too, that the massive city wall was constructed, partly to protect Visby's German merchants from attacks by the peasant-traders out in the countryside. These German merchants had close connections with the Hanseatic League in Lübeck. It was therefore natural that the German Church of St. Maria, now Visby cathedral, and likewise the big mercantile buildings, should incorporate vast attics serving as storerooms.

Gotland may have been a wealthy island at the beginning of the Middle Ages, but by the end it had become very impoverished. During the forthcoming centuries, Danish and Swedish rulers were to exhaust the island's resources. It is understandable that the Gotlanders have always preferred to manage their own affairs. Today Gotland has no great monetary riches. The busy trading vessels of the past have been replaced by tourist ferries and souvenirs are now being sold instead of tar, salt and hops. But the wealth of an ancient culture and a generous nature is something which Gotland can never lose.

Der Schafstamm ist der größte des Landes, und das Fleisch der Lämmer, die hier draußen auf den salzgesättigten Wiesen weiden, bekommt einen Geschmack, der sich nicht mit anderem Lammfleisch vergleichen läßt. Vielleicht liegt das auch zum Teil an den wildwachsenden Kräutern, die das Fleisch würzen.

Genauso aktuell wie das heutige Leben auf der Insel ist Gotlands Vorzeit. Nirgendwo anders in Schweden kann man so viele und reiche Überreste aus der Vorzeit aufweisen wie auf Gotland. Man glaubt zu wissen, daß die Insel um 5000 v. Chr. besiedelt wurde. Die vielen Schiffsetzungen zeigen, daß die Insulaner ein seefahrendes Volk waren, und schon während der römischen Eisenzeit war Gotland eine der führenden Handelsmächte in der Ostsee.

Die Insel wurde im 12. Jahrhundert christianisiert, und man führte ein reiches Leben mit eigenen Gesetzen und eigener Rechtsprechung. "Gutalagen" zählt zu den ältesten Provinzgesetzen.

Trotz seiner reichen Vorzeit ist das frühe Mittelalter und vor allen Dingen das 13. Jahrhundert Gotlands Blütezeit. Damals wurden die meisten der Kirchen auf der Insel gebaut, fast alle in gotischer Art mit Stein- und Holzskulpturen, Kalkgemälden und Inventar in ungewöhnlichem Reichtum.

Damals baute man auch die gewaltige Wehrmauer, die die deutschen Kaufleute der Stadt vor Angriffen von den freien Handelsbauern auf dem Lande schützen sollte. Die deutschen Kaufleute hatten eine starke Anknüpfung an die Hanse in Lübeck. Deshalb war es ganz natürlich, daß man die deutsche Kirche St. Maria, die heute Domkirche ist, und ebenso die großen Handelshäuser mit riesigen Dachböden ausrüstete, die als Lager dienen konnten.

Während die Insel zu Anfang des Mittelalters reich war, so war sie am Ende dieses Zeitalters völlig verarmt. Dänische und schwedische Herren sollten unter folgenden Jahrhunderten die Insel arm machen.

Gotland kann in der heutigen Zeit seinen Reichtum nicht in Geld zählen. Die großen Handelsschiffe sind gegen Touristenfähren ausgetauscht, und anstatt Teer, Salz und Hopfen verkauft man Souvenire. Aber den Schätzen der alten Kultur und einer großzügigen Natur sind die modernen Zeiten kann überlegen.

Visby –
a city by the sea

Visby –
die Stadt am Meer

There was quite certainly no such thing as tourists during the Stone Age, but the idea is an interesting one. Imagine paddling up in a hollowed-out log to the Visby of that time, reaching its shoreline, much farther inland than it is today. In fact the Stone Age shoreline would have been somewhere around present-day Mellangatan which is the middle one of three parallel streets in modern Visby.

The Stone Age village has not yet been named Visby and is located in the northern part of today's city centre. Small huts huddle under the cliffside seeking shelter from the elements and the people tending their fires here

Ganz sicher gab es in der Steinzeit keine Touristen, aber es ist spannend, mit dem Gedanken zu spielen. Sich in einem ausgehöhlten Eichenbaumstamm dem damaligen Visby zu nähern und sich an die Strandkante gleiten zu lassen, die bedeutend höher liegt als heute, ungefähr in gleicher Höhe mit Mellangatan, der mittleren der drei Parallelstraßen.

Den Namen Visby hat es noch nicht, und das Dorf liegt da, wo sich heute der nördliche Teil der Innenstadt ausbreitet. Kleine Hütten verkriechen sich zum Schutz gegen Wind und Wetter unter das Kalkplateau, und die

6

Fiskargränd is one of Visby's most popular little lanes, delighting sightseers and photographers alike with its magnificent roses and tiny houses.

Die Fischergasse wird oft besucht, geliebt von Spaziergängern und Fotografen wegen ihrer hübschen Rosen und malerischen Häuser.

Visby, known as the city of roses and ruins, also has a busy smallcraft harbour. Many visitors prefer to come to the island in their own boat.

Visby, die Stadt der Rosen und Ruinen, hat auch einen vielbesuchten Bootshafen für Freizeitboote. Viele Menschen ziehen es vor, im eigenen Boot zur Insel zu kommen.

Stora Torget and the St Karin's ruins.

Der große Marktplatz mit der Kirche Santa Karin.

appear fairly contented. The sea is bountiful and there is a good supply of fresh water. To the south of the village is what is called a flush marsh which provides fresh water and also affords a certain protection against unwelcome visitors.

Now let us return again, in the 13th century this time, aboard one of the many trading vessels coming into Visby. The city is flourishing as never before. The port is open to trade and thronging with merchants from all over Europe. By now the shoreline has retreated to about Almedalen and from the harbour one cannot fail to be impressed by

Menschen scheinen es recht schön zu haben an ihren Feuern. Das Meer ist großzügig, und es gibt ausreichend frisches Wasser. Südlich vom Dorf liegt ein sogenanntes Berieselungsmoor, das sowohl Süßwasser als auch einen gewissen Schutz gegen unwillkommene Besucher gibt.

Fahren wir zurück in das 13. Jahrhundert mit einem der vielen Handelsschiffe, die Visby besuchen. Die Stadt erlebt eine Blütezeit ohnegleichen. Der Hafen ist frei für Handel, und hier drängen sich Kaufleute aus ganz Europa. Die Strandkante befindet sich jetzt in der Höhe von Almedalen. Vom Hafen aus gesehen, kann man es

Visby centre was one of the pilot projects in the UN 1975 European Architectural Heritage Year. The Mahogny Villa in Mellangatan is one of the many protected historical buildings.

Die Innenstadt von Visby war eines der wegweisenden Projekte im europäischen Baudenkmalpflegejahr der Vereinten Nationen 1975. Das Mahagoni-Haus an Mellangatan ist nur eines der vielen Häuser, die unter Denkmalschutz stehen.

Visby is built on a slope and has narrow streets and lanes. A walk here means good exercise too.

Visby liegt an einem Hang und hat schmale Straßen und Gassen. Ein Spaziergang gibt Bewegung.

Gamla Apoteket in Strandgatan was originally a mediaeval warehouse, much later becoming an apothecary's premises. It is now converted into modern flats.

Gamla Apoteket an Strandgatan ist ein mittelalterliches Speicherhaus, das erst viel später als Apotheke verwendet wurde. Heute sind in dem Haus moderne Wohnungen eingerichtet.

10

Strandgatan's many mercantile houses with their stepped gables facing the sea. In all probability many of the visitors have never before seen such big buildings. The city, founded by the Germans, is built on the drained marsh and Strandgatan, the main thoroughfare, has more the appearance of an open marketplace.

The most imposing building of all, of course, is the 8-storey warehouse; called Liljehornska huset, today known as one of the tallest of the surviving mediaeval buildings apart from the churches. Kegs of fish, seal meat and tar were rolled out through the gates, in exchange for incoming silks, brocades and similar fineries from the Hanseatic towns on the other side of the Baltic Sea.

The Clematis House and Gamla Apoteket on Strandgatan are likewise former warehouses. A number of these Strandgatan buildings still have their trade doors and goods elevator fixtures.

Visby city wall was first built facing the sea to secure the city from outside attack. But when it subsequently emerged that the rural peasants were becoming increasingly hostile to the city merchants it was decided to extend the wall along that side too. The city wall was built in the 13th and 14th centuries and with a length of 3½ km. it is one of Europe's largest mediaeval structures. Visby's oldest building altogether is Kruttornet at Fiskarporten, a watchtower believed to be from the 12th century.

Central Visby contains numerous ruins of mediaeval churches and monasteries. There is said to have been seventeen of these originally but today only one remains intact: St Maria's, the German merchants' church which is now the Visby diocese cathedral. The ruins of the church of St Nicholas are fairly well preserved and are used for a few weeks each summer as the setting for Petrus de Dacia's Ruin Pageant. This is a dramatic presentation of the Dominican Prior's life history told in song. It is said that the two beautiful rose-windows in the west front of St. Nicholas Church originally incorporated cabochon garnets or carbuncles. These precious stones were apparently seized, however, in 1361 when the Danish King Waldemar Atterdag invaded Gotland and plundered Visby. Waldemar Atterdag benefitted little from this expedition though, for his treasure ship, bound for Denmark, foundered off the Karlsö islands − something which has capti-

nicht vermeiden, sich von den vielen Handelshäusern entlang der Strandgata beeindrucken zu lassen, die ihre hohen Staffelgiebel zum Meer wenden. Ganz sicher haben viele Besucher noch niemals vorher so große Häuser gesehen. Die Stadt, die von Deutschen angelegt wurde ist, liegt auf dem jetzt trockengelegten Berieselungsmoor. Strandgatan, die Paradestraße der Stadt, sieht hauptsächlich wie ein offener Marktplatz aus.

Am meisten imponiert natürlich das acht Stockwerke hohe Speicherhaus, das man heute das Liljehornska Haus nennt. Es dürfte eines der höchsten bewahrten mittelalterlichen Gebäude sein, Kirchen nicht eingerechnet. Fässer mit Fisch, Robbenfleisch und Teer wurden aus den Toren gerollt, getauscht gegen Seide, Brokat und andere prächtige Schmuckgegenstände aus den Hansestädten an der anderen Seite der Ostsee.

Auch das Clematis-Haus und Gamla Apoteket sind alte Speicherhäuser an der Strandgata, wo man noch heute an einigen Häusern intakte Lieferanteneingänge und Lastenaufzüge sehen kann.

Die Stadtmauer von Visby wurde zunächst zur Meeresseite hin gebaut, um die Stadt gegen Angriffe von außen zu schützen. Aber als es sich allmählich zeigte, daß die Bauern auf dem Lande sich nicht mit den Kaufleuten in der Stadt vertrugen, wurde die Mauer auch gegen die Landseite hin weiter ausgebaut. Die Stadtmauer wurde im 13. und 14. Jahrhundert gebaut und gehört mit einer Länge von ca. 3,5 km zu Europas größten mittelalterlichen Bauwerken. Das älteste bewahrte Bauwerk der Stadt ist der Pulverturm beim Fiskarport (Fischertor), einem Wachturm, von dem man annimmt, daß er im 12. Jahrhundert gebaut wurde.

Wandert man in der Innenstadt von Visby umher, so sieht man überall die Ruinen von Kirchen und Klöstern. Von den siebzehn mittelalterlichen Kirchen und Klöstern, die es einmal in der Stadt gegeben haben soll, ist nur Santa Maria, die Kirche der deutschen Kaufleute, übriggeblieben, heute Domkirche im Visby Stift. Ziemlich gut bewahrt ist die Ruine St. Nicolai, die man für ein paar Wochen im Sommer für das Ruinenspiel Petrus de Dacia benutzt − eine dramatische Wiedergabe der literären Lebensgeschichte des Priors, die mit schönem Gesang in der Klosterschule der schwarzen Brüder wiedergegeben

vated fishermen and treasure-hunters eversince.

St. Karin's or St. Katarina's is a beautiful ruin at Stora Torget; graceful arches silhouetted against a blue sky or a pale pink twilight, the ancient remains of a venerable Franciscan monastery church.

No visitor should miss Visby's botanical gardens, created at the close of the last century by a group of gentlemen who customarily met to bathe in the sea at Snäckviken, north of Visby. "De Badande Wännerna", i.e. "The Bathing Friends", as the society is still called, bought this ground on the outskirts of the city and since then the site has matured into verdant, exotic gardens cherished by natives and visitors alike.

Burmeisterska huset and Donners plats in Visby are both deserving of a visit. Burmeisterska huset, now the premises of the Tourist Centre and homecraft shop, was built in the 17th century by the wealthy merchant Hans Burmeister. On the first floor there are a number of beautiful rooms with the original murals — biblical and hunting scenes — by Johan Målare, a German-born painter. Burmeister, like the Donner merchant family, was from Lübeck.

The post office, a yellow-coloured stone building at Donners plats, is a mediaeval mercantile house.

Yet another interesting building in Visby is the Gotland Fornsal in the old aquavit distillery on Strandgatan. This is one of Sweden's finest provincial museums, containing the many treasures found in the Gotland humus and presenting a broad compendium of the island's ancient culture.

St. Maria's Church.

Die Kirche Santa Maria.

wird. In den zierlichen Rosettenfenstern an der westlichen Giebelwand sollen der Sage nach rote Karfunkel eingefaßt gewesen sein. Die leuchtenden Edelsteine sind allerdings bei der Plünderung im Jahre 1361 verlorengegangen, als der dänische König Waldemar Atterdag die Reichtümer der Bürger sehr hart anging. Er bekam jedoch seine Strafe, als das Schiff mit dem Schatz bei den Karlsinseln sank, was in allen Zeiten sowohl Fischer als auch Schatzsucher fasziniert hat.

Die hübsche Ruine beim großen Marktplatz heißt Santa Karin oder Katarina. Mit einer Eleganz, würdig einer Primadonna, hebt sie ihre schlanken Gewölbebögen zum blauen Himmel empor, und mit dem rosa Zwielicht in den ergrauten Zügen geht die gråbrödramunkarnas klosterkyrka (Klosterkirche der Graubrüder-Mönche) einem schönen Alter entgegen.

Zu einem Spaziergang in Visby gehört eine Pause im Botanischen Garten. Er ist eine Schöpfung der Herren, die sich Ende des vorigen Jahrhunderts versammelten, um unter ausgelassener Fröhlichkeit in der Schneckenbucht nördlich der Stadt zu baden. "De badande Wännerna" "Die badenden Freunde", wie die Gesellschaft noch heute heißt, ließ das Gelände am Rande der Stadt, wo der Garten liegt, aufkaufen. Im Laufe der Jahrzehnte hat sich der Garten zu einem dichtbelaubten exotischen Wäldchen entwickelt, das Inselbewohnern und auch Touristen Abkühlung und Enstspannung bietet.

Als Besucher in Visby sollte man unbedingt sowohl das Burmeister-Haus als auch Donner-Platz besichtigen. Das Burmeister-Haus, in dem heute das Fremdenverkehrsbüro und das gotländische Heimatwerk (Hemslöjd) Platz hat, wurde im 17. Jahrhundert von dem Großkaufmann Hans Burmeister erbaut. Im ersten Stockwerk sind hübsche Räume bewahrt, in denen der Künstler der Stadt, Johan Målare, die Wände mit biblischen Motiven und prachtvollen Jagdszenen dekoriert hat.

Genau wie Burmeister, kam auch die Kaufmannsfamilie Donner aus Lübeck. Wer das Postamt in dem gelben Steinhaus am Donner-Platz besucht, besucht gleichzeitig das mittelalterliche Kaufmannshaus.

Gotlands Fornsal (Landesmuseum), das in der alten Schnapsbrennerei an Strandgatan liegt, ist einer der schönsten Provinzmuseen des Landes.

The Gotland winter is usually mild, but sometimes the snow comes, delighting the children in particular.

Auf Gotland ist der Winter mild, aber ab und zu fällt Schnee und gibt den Kindern Gelegenheit zu winterlichen Spielen.

Winter imbues the city with the beauty of an engraving. To seaward the snowclouds roll by, while pale street lighting throws a yellow glow over the great wall.

Im Winter ist die Stadt von graphischer Schönheit. Schneewolken ziehen vorbei über das Meer, und das bleiche Licht einer Straßenlaterne verbreitet einen gelblichen Schimmer über die Mauer.

On the first Sunday of Advent there is a Christmas Fair at Stora Torget. From the tower of the cathedral Visby then looks like a lilliput town.

Am ersten Advents-Sonntag findet der Weihnachtsmarkt auf dem großen Marktplatz statt. Vom Turm der Domkirche aus sieht Visby dann aus wie eine Spielzeugstadt.

Looking north from the cathedral tower we see the City Wall with Norderport and the ruins of St. Göran, the latter once a hospital for lepers.

Vom Turm der Domkirche sieht man im Norden die Stadtmauer mit Norderport und die Ruinen von St. Göran, wo früher einmal ein Krankenhaus für Lepra-Kranke eingerichtet war.

Shoreline

Strandgebiet

Gotland has many sandy beaches, but there are also stony coastlines where the only colour may be provided by briar rose blooms.

Es gibt viele Sandstrände auf Gotland, aber auch steinige Küsten, wo nur die Blüten der wilden Heckenrosen der grauen Landschaft Farbe verleihen.

Abandoned, frost-powdered beach slippers, provoking memories of a summer past and anticipation of a summer coming . . .

Ein gefrorener Badeschuh, mit Reiffrost gepudert, liegt vergessen als Erinnerung an den Sommer, der vorbei ist und die Sehnsucht nach warmen Tagen weckt.

Searching for fossils is a popular pastime. But one should be prudent and considerate, the Swedish common right of access to private land also implies a proper respect for these unique surroundings.

Es ist sehr beliebt, nach Fossilien zu suchen. Aber der Strandboden verlangt Achtsamkeit. Das schwedische "Allemansrätt" (Recht zum Gemeinbrauch) verlangt auch gleichzeitig, die Natur nicht zu zerstören.

In wintertime the shore is frozen and the seaweed crackles under your feet. But it is still a lovely time for a walk, when the sun casts pale shadows...

Im Winter liegt der Strand gefroren, und der Tang knirscht unter den Schuhen. Die Sonne wirft bleiche Schatten, aber trotzdem ist der Strand ein schönes Ausflugsziel.

Even a landscape in grey has a certain strange beauty, offering spiritual repose...

Auch eine Landschaft ganz in Grau ist schön und erholsam.

The long, long sandy beaches encourage great projects. And isn't it splendid when there is enough sand to just keep on building . . .?

Die breiten Sandstrände fordern geradezu zum Spielen heraus, und es ist sicher herrlich, wenn es Sand genug gibt für alles, was man machen will.

Meadows of heaven

Himmlische
Wiesen

A Gotland meadow is sheer delight for flower-lovers. Rare orchids commingle here with all the common flowers of the field, while round about the leafy treetops dapple the ground with lively shadow.

The meadow is the farmer's joy; a pastoral haven after the labours of the day. In the past for smallholders the meadow also provided hay and other fodder for the domestic animals. Nowadays volunteers often help keep the meadows in trim. They must be raked in the spring, scythed in the summer and cleaned out in the winter.

Certain of the large meadowlands like Hammars, Mästerbyänget, Alvena Lindaränge, Allekvia and Mangsarve

Ein gotländisches äng (Art Lichtung im Laubwald) ist ein Paradies für den Blumenfreund. Hier vermischen sich eine Vielzahl von Orchideen mit gewöhnlichen Sommerblumen, und die Baumkronen legen einen Schimmer über den Laubsaal.

Der äng ist der Stolz des Bauern. Ein Platz, wo man sich erholen kann von den Strapazen des Alltags, nur um die einzigartige Schönheit des äng zu genießen. Während der Zeit der Naturhaushaltung brachte der äng auch Heu und Laub für die Tiere ein. Heute helfen viele Freiwillige mit, den äng am Leben zu halten. Er soll im Frühjahr gehackt werden, im Sommer wird Heu geerntet, und im Winter

are cared for by naturelovers and homestead organizations and everyone is welcome to these to experience the rapture of the Gotland summer.

muß gelichtet werden zwischen den Bäumen, damit der äng nicht verwahrlost.

Es gibt Bauern, die die ängen auf ihren Höfen nur ihrer Schönheit wegen intakthalten. Einige große ängen, wie Hammars, Mästerbyänget, Alvena Lindaränget, Allekvis und Mangsarve werden von Naturfreunden und Heimatvereinen bewahrt, und jeder ist herzlich willkommen, dort den herrlichen gotländischen Sommer zu genießen.

Haymaking is the culmination of the summer. Everyone lends a hand now to nurture and preserve the meadow.

Die Heuernte bildet den Höhepunkt des Sommers. Dann versammeln sich alle und helfen mit, den äng am Leben zu halten.

In the early summer sweet-smelling meadow saxifrage peeps up through the grass, followed shortly after by the orchids and a myriad other summer flowers.

Im Vorsommer schauen die duftenden weißen Mandelblüten aus dem Gras hervor. Bald folgen ihnen Orchideen und Sommerblumen.

Even the very smallest takes part in the work and many willing arms are needed, for the meadow must never be exposed to mechanical devices.

Auch die Jüngsten nehmen an der Arbeitsgemeinschaft teil. Man braucht viele Freiwillige, denn der äng kann nicht auf moderne Art und Weise bewirtschaftet werden.

Following page
Lady's slipper (Cypripedium calceolus) is one of the most majestic of the orchids. Like most of its kin, it is protected.

Folgende Seite
Der Frauenschuh zählt zu den prächtigsten Orchideen. Genauso wie viele andere seiner Art steht er unter Naturschutz.

Nature's poorhouse

Das Armenhaus
der Natur

It is difficult to believe that the machines have spared something in our day and age. Nevertheless they have — they have overlooked the moorland, that meagre ground, nature's poorhouse where twisted pines, scanty juniper and mosses struggle to survive. The moorland is dramatic in its indigence and nowhere else does the tiniest wild flower gleam so brightly as against this ruptured limestone.

Yet some flowers seem to thrive here despite the sparseness of the soil and the moorland thus yields many rare and exquisite summer blooms.

But the most beautiful moment of all is still to tramp the sheep trails when the air is clear and keen and the crimson shades of autumn are emerging. The yellowing grass sways forlornly now and the wind caresses the late flowers, lamenting the passing of the Swedish summer.

Es ist merkwürdig, daß irgendetwas in unserer Zeit von Maschinen verschont geblieben ist; und trotzdem: die Maschinen haben die Heide übersehen. Den kargen, steinigen Boden, das Armenhaus der Natur, wo verkrüppelte Kiefern, Wacholder und Moose für ihren Lebensunterhalt kämpfen. Die Heide ist dramatisch in ihrer Armut, und nirgendwo anders erhält die kleinste Blumenblüte eine so starke Leuchtkraft wie gegen den aufgerissenen Kalkstein gesehen.

Viele Blumen scheinen jedoch Nachsicht zu üben mit dem dürftigen Erdvorrat, und die Heide beschehrt uns hübsche Sommerblumen den ganzen Sommer über.

Das Schönste ist doch, auf den ausgetrampelten Stiegen der Lämmer zu wandern, wenn die Luft klar und hell ist und das Laub anfängt sich rot zu färben. Dann weht das gelbe Gras, dann singen die Blumen des Windes ein Abschiedslied an den schwedischen Sommer.

When yellow bedstraw arrays the moorland in gold there is a scent of honey. The open-pasture sheep are accustomed to the meagre grazing.

Es riecht nach Honig, wenn das gelbe Waldstroh die Heide in Gelb kleidet. Die Schafe, die das ganze Jahr im Freien grasen, sind das magere Futter gewohnt.

White sedum seems to grow out of the very rock. These blooms are suitable for making dried flowers.

Anscheinend völlig ohne Erde wächst weiße Fetthenne auf den grauen Felsenplatten. Sie läßt sich auch als Trockenblume verwenden.

In the middle of the summer the lavender-hued chive spreads like a cloud across the moorland. This, too, can be dried for winter bouquets.

Mitten im Sommer zieht der violett blühende Schnittlauch wie eine Wolke über die Heide. Auch er kann für Winterblumensträuße getrocknet werden.

Ivy is Gotland's floral emblem, but it is the rich hues of blueweed, or viper's bugloss, that lends character to the countryside.

Gotlands Provinz-Blume ist das Efeu. Aber charakteristisch für die Provinz ist die hervorstechende Armee des leuchtenden blauen Heinrich.

There are no "sheep" on Gotland

Es gibt keine Schafe auf Gotland

The sheep are called "lambs" and the small lambs "young lambs". They are born black, maturing to become grey with a black head.

Die Schafe auf der Insel nennt man Lämmer, und ihre Jungen die kleinen Lämmchen. Neugeborene sind schwarz, die ausgewachsenen Tiere sind grau und haben schwarze Köpfe.

One man *can* manage a large flock of sheep — assisted by his dog which does the job of several more men.

Ein Mann kann allein eine große Lammherde versorgen, aber sein Hirtenhund ist eine unschätzbare Hilfe und ersetzt mehrere Arbeitskräfte.

The dog looks attentively up at his master — time to run the flock together?

Der Hund schaut aufmerksam zu seinem Herrchen — ist es Zeit, die Herde zusammenzutreiben?

Hurry – Hurry – spindly black legs beat the frozen ground as they hasten towards the feed-shed.

Schnell, schnell – dünne schwarze Beine trommeln über den gefrorenen Boden zum "gedeckten Tisch".

Perhaps it was a lingering memory of summer which urged these sheep to form this floral pattern . . .

War es vielleicht die Sehnsucht nach den Sommerwiesen, die diese hübsche "Schafblume" hervorbrachte?

orland is well suited to sheep farming. But the sheep need
ty of space for they have to change their grazing ground
uently if they are to stay healthy.

Der Heideboden eignet sich gut für Schafzucht. Es wird sehr viel Land gebraucht, denn die Lämmer müssen oft die Weiden wechseln um gesund zu bleiben.

Church
of the Twelve Peasants
— and a few others

Die "Zwölf-Bauern-
Kirche"
und noch einige mehr

Gammelgarn church in the eastern part of Gotland adjoins a well-preserved 12th century defensive tower.

These motifs from The Fall of Man over the nave portal are the work of the stone carver "Egypticus".

Die Kirche von Gammelgarn, auf der Ostseite der Insel, wird von einem gut erhaltenen Kastal (Verteidigungsturm) aus dem 12. Jahrhundert flankiert.

Die Bilder aus dem "Sündenfall" über dem Eingang zum Längs-Schiff sind das Werk des Steinmetzes "Egypticus".

It would be difficult to find more mediaeval churches assembled in an area smaller than that of Gotland. Of all the churches in use today on the island ninety or more are mediaeval.

Most of the Gotland churches were built at a time when the islanders were free trader peasants doing business all over the known world. A great many churches were erected during this era of prosperity when a wealthy peasant would have his own church built, for personal prestige or possibly because he considered it too far to the nearest place of worship.

Perhaps the most remarkable thing about these Gotland churches, meanwhile, is not so much their survival as the fact that they contain such a wealth of ecclesiastical art. The trader peasants observed and absorbed in other lands and thus the church art on Gotland was often manifestly influenced by the work of artists of distant provenance.

But with the advent of the Hanseatic League and the arrival of the German merchants in Visby the prosperity of the Gotland peasants came to an end. This brought to a

Es ist sicher schwierig, mehr mittelalterliche Kirchen auf einem so begrenzten Gebiet wie Gotland zu finden. Von den Kirchen, die heute noch benutzt werden, stammen ca. 90 aus dem Mittelalter. Dazu kommen die verlassenen Kirchen, wie die Kirchenruine von Gann, wo man jedes Jahr die Mittsommernachtmesse abhält, mit dem Himmel als Kirchendach.

Die meisten der Kirchen auf der Insel wurden zu der Zeit gebaut, als die Gotländer freie Handelsbauern waren mit Verbindungen über die ganze damals bekannte Welt. Der reichen Zeit folgten viele Kirchen nach, denn wer den Weg zur Kirche zu weit fand, oder sich auf die eine oder andere Weise hervortun wollte, konnte sich eine eigene Kirche bauen.

Das Merkwürdigste ist vielleicht doch nicht, daß die Kirchen bis heute erhalten sind, sondern, daß so viele von ihnen einen Kunstschatz innehaben, der sich mit Europas meist bekannter Kirchenkunst vergleichen läßt. Ursprünglich waren die Kirchen noch viel mehr ausgeschmückt. Die gotländische Kirchenkunst hat oft ihre Vor-

Stånga church tower is one of the tallest on the island. The composition of the sculpture groups around the nave portal has bewildered art historians for centuries.

Der Turm von Stånga Kirche ist einer der höchsten auf der Insel. Die Komposition am Mittelschiff-Portal hat die Kunsthistoriker zu allen Zeiten verblüfft.

This gilded, enthroned Viklau madonna is a 12th century wood sculpture. The original is in the National Historical Museum in Stockholm while there are copies in Viklau church and in Gotlands Fornsal.

Die vergoldete Viklau-Madonna auf ihrem Thron ist eine Holzskulptur aus dem 12. Jahrhundert. Das Original steht im staatlichen Naturhistorischen Museum in Stockholm und Nachbildungen in der Kirche von Viklau und in Gotlands Fornsal.

The abstractly decorated triumphial arch in Vallstena church seems somehow out of place on Gotland. The inspiration for this doubtless derived from far afield.

Der abstrakt gemusterte Triumphbogen in der Kirche von Vallstena sieht nicht so aus, als ob er von Gotland stamme. Sicher hat man Inspiration dazu weit weg von zuhause gesucht.

The stained glass in Lye church is part of Scandinavia's largest extant suite of mediaeval stained glass.

Die Glasfenster in der Kirche von Lye gehören zu der größten bewahrten Serie mittelalterlicher Glasmalereien in den nordischen Ländern.

halt not only the building of churches but also the development of church art. The severe doctrines of the Reformation almost gave the final blow to the old art treasures. Decorative work was no longer permitted in church interiors. The more zealous officials had paintings and sculptures done away with altogether. Others contented themselves with decreeing that the beautiful frescoes and ceiling pieces should be obliterated by limewash, thereby inadvertently conserving these unique treasures for posterity.

Many of the Gotland churches contain work by mediaeval stone carvers. These were anonymous craftsmen whom art historians have since endowed with such pseudonyms as Byzantios, Majestatis, Egypticus and Fabulator. Their work includes portals, friezes and fonts.

Most of the churches are worth a visit. Here is a selection of what is to be seen in a few of them.

Hejdeby church, east of Visby, is as picturesque as a child's cutout model for a toy village. The walls are blandly white while the black-tarred tower rises sternly towards the heavens. This is a small building, sometimes referred to as the "Church of The Twelve Peasants". The frescoes inside are probably 13th century, the work of one Michael the Master (Mikaelsmästaren). The font has a finely carved wooden lid in the design of a cruciform church.

Stånga church in the southeast has an interesting nave portal. Most of the sculptures are assembled in groups to the right of the portal while isolated at the apex of the interrupted gable is the figure of the resurrected Christ. Art historians have been unable to offer any explanation for this erratic composition.

Vallstena church, east of Visby, contains a 13th century triumphal arch elaborately decorated in abstract patterns which seem entirely foreign to our latitudes. The paintings are well-preserved and have never been limewashed over.

Gammalgarn church is also to the east of Visby. Adjacent to it is an imposing 12th century defensive tower with interesting stone relief work over the portals. The motifs here include Noah's Ark and the Creation.

In *Burs church* the choir pews are carved from limestone with biblical scenes on the abundantly ornamented pew ends. There is still a certain amount of well-preserved

bilder von weit außerhalb der Landesgrenzen geholt.

Als die Hanse kam war es aus mit den Reichtümern für die Bauern. Da stockten sowohl Kirchenbau als auch die Möglichkeit, die Kirchenkunst weiterzuentwickeln. Sicherlich war das nicht nur zu beklagen. Vielleicht hätte sonst die frühmittelalterliche Kunst einer moderneren Ausschmückung weichen müssen. Die strengen Lehren der Reformation gaben den alten Kunstschätzen fast den Todesstoß. War man dienstbeflissen, so wurden die Malereien und Skulpturen vollkommen zerstört, an manchen Stellen gab man sich damit zufrieden, die hübschen Malereien nur zu weißen. Aber unter den weiß getünchten Wänden wurde ein einmaliger Kunstschatz für die Nachwelt bewahrt.

Die gotländischen Kirchen sind oft mit den Werken von mittelalterlichen Steinmetzen ausgeschmückt. Da sie für die Nachwelt unbekannt sind, haben Kunsthistoriker ihnen erfundene Namen verliehen, wie Byzantios, Majestatis, Egypticus. Zu ihren Werken zählen z. B. Portale, Friesen und Taufbecken.

So gut wie jede gotländische Kirche ist einen Besuch wert, und es ist schwierig, die eine der anderen vorzuziehen. Aber da deren Anzahl so groß ist, wollen wir wenigstens eine Kostprobe geben.

Die Kirche von Hejdeby, östlich von Visby gelegen. Die Kirche ist klein und wird manchmal "Tolv bönders kyrka" "Zwölf-Bauern-Kirche" genannt. In der Kirche kann man fein abgestimmte Kalkgemälde sehen, wahrscheinlich im 13. Jahrhundert angefertigt von dem sogenannten Mikaels-Meister (Mikaelsmästaren). Hier gibt es auch ein Taufbecken mit einem hübsch geschnitzten Holzdeckel in Form einer Kreuzkirche.

Die Kirche von Stånga im Südosten hat ein interessantes Mittelschiff-Portal. Eine Menge Skulpturen sind in Gruppen auf der rechten Seite vom Portal angesammelt, und ganz oben in dem aufgebrochenen Wimperg sitzt der auferstandene Christus. Warum das Portal diese verwirrte Komposition erhalten hat, ist den Kunsthistorikern ein Rätsel geblieben.

In der Kirche von Vallstena, östlich von Visby, gibt es einen Triumphbogen aus dem 13. Jahrhundert, reich dekoriert mit einem abstrakten Muster, das für unsere Breitengrade ganz fremd wirkt. Die Malereien sind gut

colour here, which suggests that many of the stone sculptures may originally have been painted.

Lye church, to the south, possesses some fine mediaeval stained glass. It is remarkable that this delicate work should have survived so many periods of unrest and violence.

Öja church is also to the south and contains the "Mater Dolorosa" wood carving in its original surroundings. This madonna is a sidepiece to the renowned 13th century Öja crucifix and the profound sadness expressed in her finely-chiselled countenance has made her one of Sweden's most famous sculptures. Although this is otherwise the original group, the "Mater Dolorosa" here is nevertheless a replica, the original sculpture being in the Gotlands Fornsal museum in Visby.

Gerum church in the southwest is a little gem with a delightful interior incorporating frescoes from various periods. There is also an imposing 12th century font by the stone carver Majestatis.

Bro church is north of Visby; an ancient sacrificial church with interesting stone carvings from different periods.

Martebo church also has handsome stone relief work over the portals. The motif so delicately carved above the chancel portal is the "Flight into Egypt".

Going north one passes *Tingstäde church* with its very grand exterior, *Lärbro church* with a fine detached watch tower, *Bunge church* with beautiful frescoes, and finally *Fårö church* with the splendid "kuta picture" shown on the opposite page. A naive yet elaborate portrayal of sealhunters thanking the Lord for delivering them from certain death out on the ice.

erhalten und waren niemals getüncht.

Auch die Kirche von Gammelgarn liegt im Osten. Sie wird von einem prächtigen Kastal (Verteidigungsturm) aus dem 12. Jahrhundert flankiert und hat interessante Steinreliefe über den Portalen. Hier werden die Arche Noah und die Schöpfungsgeschichte in deftiger Bildsprache wiedergegeben.

In Burs großer Kirche muß man sich unbedingt die Chorbank ansehen, aus Kalkstein gehauen mit biblischen Szenen auf den reich ornamentierten Seitenstücken. Die Farbe ist zum Teil bewahrt, was darauf schließen läßt, daß viele Steinskulpturen ursprünglich angemalt gewesen sein können.

An der Kirche von Lye im Süden sollte man nicht vorbeigehen, ohne sich Zeit zu nehmen, die hübschen mittelalterlichen Glasmalereien zu bewundern. Glas ist ja ein vergängliches Material, und es ist phantastisch, daß die Gemälde in der Kirche von Lye alle unruhigen Zeiten überlebt haben.

Ganz weit im Süden findet man die Kirche von Öja. Wer die Holzskulptur "Mater Dolorosa" in ihrem ursprünglichen Milieu sehen will, kommt hierher. Die Madonna macht eine Seitenfigur zu dem berühmten Öja-Kruzifix aus dem 13. Jahrhundert aus. Ihr feingeschnittenes Gesicht drückt unendliche Wehmut aus, und das hat sie zu den berühmtesten Frauenskulpturen des Landes gemacht. Das Original befindet sich in Gotlands Fornsal in Visby.

Die Kirche von Gerum im Südwesten hat ein Taufbecken aus dem 12. Jahrhundert von dem Steinmetz Majestatis. Nördlich von Visby liegt Bro Kirche, eine alte Opferkirche mit hübschen Steinmetzarbeiten aus verschiedenen Zeitperioden.

Die Kirche von Martebo hat auch hübsche Steinreliefe über den Portalen. Über dem Chorportal findet man das Motiv "Die Flucht nach Ägypten".

Auf dem Weg nach Norden passiert man Tingstäde Kirche mit ihrem prächtigen Äußeren, Lärbro Kirche mit einem schönen Kastal, Bunge Kirche mit hübschen Kalkmalereien und schließlich Fårö Kirche mit dem fantastischen "Kuta-Tavla" (Robben-Bild). Eine volkstümliche Szene, wo ein paar Robbenfänger dem Herren für ihre Rettung vor einem sicheren Tode auf dem Eis danken.

The elaborately decorated 12th century baptismal font in Gerum church is believed to be the work of the stone carver Majestatis. The motif is the birth of Christ.

Das reich geschmückte Taufbecken in Gerums Kirche aus dem 12. Jahrhundert, wird als das Werk von Steinmetz Majestatis angesehen. Das Motiv handelt von der Geburt Jesu.

The Öja madonna is famous far beyond the frontiers of Sweden, particularly for the exquisite melancholy of her expression.

Die unendliche Wehmut in ihren blauen Augen hat die Öja-Madonna weit über die Landesgrenzen hinaus bekannt und bewundernswert gemacht.

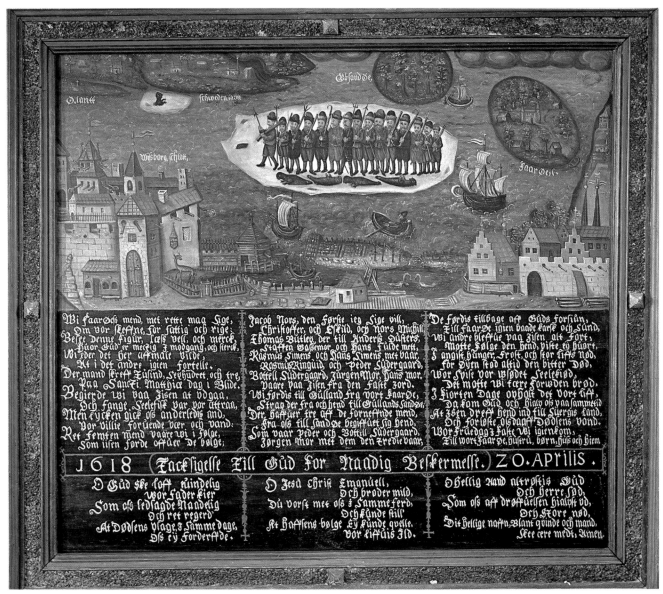

Certain death awaited the sealhunters who drifted out to sea on an ice-floe. In this picture in Fårö church they thank God for their deliverance.

Ein sicherer Tod erwartete die Robbenjäger, die auf einer Eisscholle auf das Meer hinaustrieben. Auf einem Bild in der Kirche von Fårö danken sie Gott für ihre Rettung.

A rock
in the blue haze

Die Klippe
im blauen Dunst

Lilla Karlsö

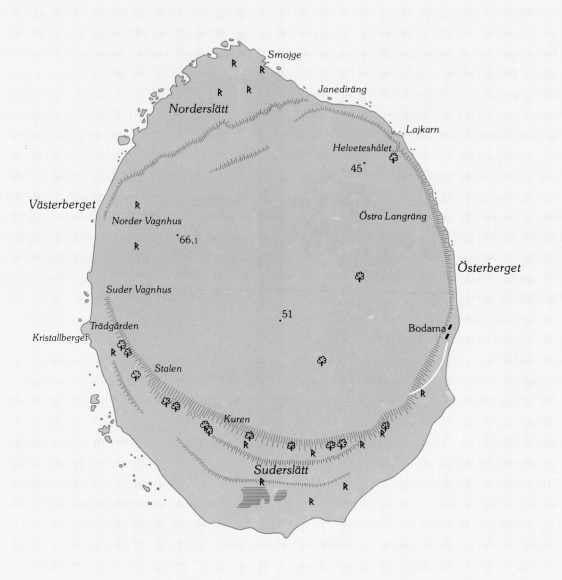

Smojge

Janediräng

Norderslätt

Lajkarn

Helveteshålet

45

Västerberget

Östra Langräng

Norder Vagnhus

66,1

Österberget

Suder Vagnhus

51

Trädgården

Bodarna

Kristallberget

Stalen

Kuren

Suderslätt

N

0   100   500 m

Sometimes on an autumn day you may catch a glimpse of Lilla Karlsö, alluring in the lead-grey distance of the sea; not quite close enough, yet not too far away. Then as the weather changes the vision fades like a shadow and you wonder to yourself whether it was ever there at all . . .

Hundreds of millions of years ago these two islands were born out of the Cambro-Silurian sea. Molluscs, mussels, corals and other alien species thrived in the tropically warm waters and it was the shells of these which formed the embryos of Stora and Lilla Karlsö.

One reaches Lilla Karlsö by boat from Klintehamn south of Visby. After barely an hour's passage the little island rises out of the sea in all its rare beauty. Gulls sweep out from the rocky cliffs, guillemots bob buoyantly among the waves and the occasional razorbill cuts like an arrow through the air. Lilla Karlsö has no permanent buildings and no natural harbour. For a month or two in the summer there is a certain amount of tourist traffic, otherwise the sheep are the lords of the island. These are a local breed known as "gute (i.e. Gotland) sheep", an ancient strain characterized by formidable curved horns, a distinctive mane and a straight but shaggy coat.

Lilla Karlsö is a little world of stone, yet it is not without colour. There are many shades of yellow and green in the dry ground. And there is grey limestone rock, talus slopes and greying trees that have lain down to die among the stones. Such trees as do grow on the island lend shade to flocks of sheep in biblical repose. The landscape altogether is barren and wild, and mostly treeless.

In the late autumn the rams and the sheep for slaughter are taken back to the mainland. Protesting loudly they are driven into pens and then shepherded aboard the boat at the pier. The most venerable of the rams is wilful and stubborn and would sooner take to the water than go aboard. New efforts are made by the drovers and finally the contrary old ram concedes, reluctantly accepting that he must leave his island harem — at least for the time being.

An bestimmten Tagen im Herbst sieht man die Insel klar und verlockend im blaugrauen Meer. Nicht nahe genug und nicht allzu weit entfernt. Wenn das Wetter umschlägt, verschwindet sie wie ein Schatten, und man zweifelt daran, ob es sie überhaupt einmal gegeben hat.

Vor ein paar hundertmillionen Jahren gebar das Kambrosilur-Meer die beiden Felseninseln hier draußen. Schnecken, Muscheln und andere fremde Arten lebten in diesem tropisch warmen Meer, und deren Schalen schufen das Embryo zu den beiden Karlsinseln.

Nach Lilla Karlsö gelangt man mit dem Boot von Klintehamn, südlich von Visby. Nach ungefähr einer Stunde Fahrt taucht die Insel wie Aphrodite aus dem Meeresschaum auf, mit ihrer ganz besonderen Schönheit.

Möwen werfen sich kreischend von den Klippen, Lummen schaukeln gemächlich auf dem Wasser, und ein paar Tordalken schießen wie Torpedos durch die Luft. Lilla Karlsö ist nicht das ganze Jahr über bewohnt, und es gibt auch keinen natürlichen Hafen. Man unterhält Touristenverkehr ein paar Monate im Sommer, die übrige Zeit beherrschen Schafe die Insel. Die Schafe, die man hier draußen hält, nennt man "gutefår" (Gotländer Schafe). Das ist eine alte Rasse, die sich durch riesige krumme Hörner, Mähnen-Kragen und glatten, zottigen Pelz kennzeichnet.

Ein Besuch auf Lilla Karlsö ist eine Wanderung in eine Steinwelt, doch nicht ohne Farberlebnisse. Der trockene Boden bietet Schattierungen in Gelb und Grün an. Graue Kalkklippen, steil abstürzende Abhänge, ergraute Bäume, die sich zum Sterben in die Steinmassen gelegt haben. Die wenigen Bäume spenden der Schafherde Schatten, in dem sie sich mit biblischer Würde ausruht. Die Landschaft ist karg und wild und bisweilen baumlos.

Im Spätherbst werden die Schafböcke und Schlachttiere auf die Höfe auf dem Land zurückgebracht. Unter lautstarken Protesten werden sie in die Gehege getrieben, und vorsichtig treiben die Männer sie an Bord des Kutters an der Landungsbrücke. Der alte Hammel ist störrisch und will lieber ins Wasser springen als an Bord gehen. Ein neuer Versuch — und zum Schluß sieht der Hammel ein, daß er sich eine Zeitlang damit abfinden muß, seinen Harem auf der Insel zu verlassen.

The path leads across impoverished moorland where the decomposing bedrock litters the sparse grass with broken stone. Here and there a tree has survived the grazing sheep flocks.

Der Pfad führt über mageren Heideboden, wo der verwitternde Felsengrund Steine ins Gras streut. Hier und da wachsen Bäume die davon verschont geblieben sind, von den Schafen abgefressen zu werden.

Sheep at rest beneath the shadow of a tree: ruminative, dignified and casually indifferent to visitors.

Die Schafherde ruht im Schatten der Bäume aus. Frei, würdig, mit zerstreut gleichgültigem Blick für den Besucher.

"Stalen" is Lilla Karlsö's tallest limestone pillar or "rauk". It rises sixteen meters towards the plateau above.

"Stalen" ist der größte rauk (Kalkklippe) der Insel. Sechzehn Meter hoch streckt er sich zum Plateau empor.

"Veite Auren" is a fine white-pebbled beach and an ideal spot for a dip in the crystal-clear water.

Umrundet man die Insel, so kommt man zu dem Geröllstrand "Veite Auren". In kristallklarem Wasser kann man hier gut baden.

Island
of legends and birds

Sagen-
und Vogelinsel

Stora Karlsö

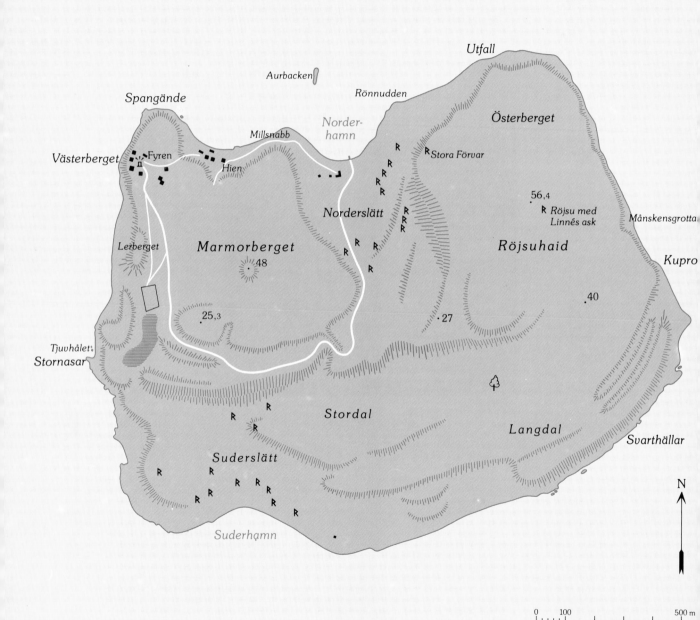

Utfall

Aurbacken

Spangände

Rönnudden

Österberget

Millsnabb

Norder-
hamn

Västerberget

Fyren

Hien

R

R

Stora Förvar

56,4

R

Röjsu med
Linnés ask

Månskensgrotta

Norderslätt

Lerberget

Marmorberget

R

R

R

Röjsuhaid

Kupro

48

R

R

.40

25,3

.27

Tjuvhålet

Stornasar

Stordal

Langdal

Svarthällar

R

R

R

Suderslätt

R

R R R

R

R R

R

Suderhamn

N

0   100   500 m

Compared with the sun-scorched grazing land of Lilla Karlsö, Stora Karlsö is a verdant bower where the broad-leaf trees are abundant and fulsome, the grass rich and green and the meadow flowers profuse. Klintehamn is likewise the point of departure for Stora Karlsö. One can spend the day on the island or stay overnight there too. The lodgings are simple and the food served at the little restaurant is plain but good. This is no Mecca for the luxury-loving traveller, but it is a paradise for the nature-lover.

Stora Karlsö is somewhat more grandiose than Lilla Karlsö. The shores reach out more gently, though in parts there is the same rocky, inaccessible coastline that is so typical of the smaller island.

Man has inhabited Stora Karlsö since the Stone Age. In the "Stora Förvar" cave, archaeologists have found implements, food remnants and ornaments from the Stone, Bronze and Iron ages. They have also come across human bones split longitudinally and scattered over the floor of the cave. Did these cavemen gorge on their brothers while the moon cast its silver sheen over the primaeval sea?

Visitors to Stora Karlsö are shown round by qualified guides, which is essential considering the rare and delicate flora and, in particular, the birdlife — for above all this is a birds' island. Thousands of great auks nest on the bird cliff on the west side of the island, thronging the rocky shelves and fishing the waters beyond. Black wings, white breasts, gaping bills, screeching bills, bills glittering silver — this is Karlsö's very own happening.

Stora Karlsö possesses many legends. Sea rovers are said to have had their hideouts here, though the most cherished legend of all is that of King Waldemar's treasure which went down off the island with the king's ship. The fishermen claim they have always known just where the treasure lies, but there is a great dog squatting on the deck hatch guarding the treasure. The only way to cheat Aegir, Master of the Seas, out of this fabulous prize is to raise twin calves on milk alone and offer these in exchange for the treasure. One such bold attempt at this was made, but it turned out that the calves had nevertheless had their noses into a bucket of water — Aegir learned of this and wrathfully demanded the return of his treasure.

Verglichen mit der sonnenverbrannten Weidelandschaft der kleinen Insel, kommt einem Stora Karlsö wie ein dicht belaubtes grünes Paradies vor. Die krausen Baumkronen bedecken steil abstürzende Abhänge und Hügel, das Gras ist saftig, und die Wiesen blühen. Nach Stora Karlsö nimmt man das Boot von Klintehamn. Man kann einen Tag auf der Insel zubringen, aber auch übernachten, auch wenn die Einquartierung einfach ist. Eine Gaststätte bietet dem Besucher einfache aber gut zubereitete Mahlzeiten an. Für den Luxus-Touristen ist dies kein Reiseziel, dafür aber für den Naturfreund.

Der Strand ist weniger abschüssig, aber an einigen Stellen findet man ähnliche unzugängliche Felsenstrände wie auf der kleinen Insel.

Seit der Steinzeit haben schon Menschen auf Stora Karlsö gewohnt. In der Grotte "Stora Förvar" haben Archäologen Werkzeuge, Nahrungsmittel und Schmuckgegenstände aus der Stein-, Bronze- und Eisenzeit gefunden. Man hat aber auch Menschenknochen gefunden, die der Länge nach aufgespalten über den Boden der Höhle verstreut lagen. Verspeiste der Höhlenmensch vielleicht seinen Bruder, während der Mond seinen silbernen Schein über das Urmeer warf? Der Höhlenboden antwortet nicht auf diese Frage.

Um Stora Karlsö herum wandert man in Begleitung eines erfahrenen Fremdenführers. Das muß sein im Hinblick auf die empfindliche Flora und nicht zuletzt der Vögel wegen, denn dies ist die Insel der Vögel. Auf dem Vogelberg im Westen brüten tausende von Alken, und die, die sich nicht auf den Klippen drängen, fischen draußen auf dem Meer. Schwarze Flügel, weiße Brust, aufgesperrte Schnäbel, Schnäbel mit Lametta versehen.

Stora Karlsö ist sagenumsponnen. Räuberbanden hatten ihre Zuflucht auf der Insel aber am meisten lockt die Sage von König Waldemars Schatz, den das Meer draußen mit Mann und Maus verschlang. Fischer haben zu allen Zeiten gewußt, wo das Schiff mit dem Schatz lag, aber auf er Lucke zum Laderaum sitzt ein großer Hund, der ihn schwer erreichbar macht. Die einzige Möglichkeit, König Ägir um seinen Schatz zu bringen, ist, ein paar Zwillingskälber nur mit Milch aufzuziehen, ohne einen Tropfen Wasser, und sie gegen den Schatz einzutauschen.

One variety of the guillemot has a characteristic white line extending out behind the eye.

Eine Trottellummenart ist mit einer weißen Augenlinie versehen.

A white breast, a black jacket and a long bill are the distinguishing features of the razorbill. Gullemots and razorbills are the principal occupants of Stora Karlsö's bird cliff.

Weiße Brust, schwarzer Frack und langer Schnabel sind das Kennzeichen für den Tordalken. Zusammen mit den Trottellummen bevölkert er den Vogelberg auf Stora Karlsö.

Far out to the west is the lighthouse, a castle-like building with a magnificent view over the Baltic.

Ganz weit draußen im Westen liegt der Leuchtturm. Ein schloßähnliches Gebäude mit herrlicher Aussicht über das freie Wasser.

Following pages
Auks in flight over the sea.

The "Stora Förvar" cave.

Folgende Seiten.
Alken über dem Meer.

Die Grotte Stora Förvar.

Seafarers' Island

Die Insel
der Seefahrer

Fårö

Raukomr.

Tällevika

Norsholmen

Skärsände

Ajkesvik

Digerhuvud

Langhammars

Norsta Auren

Helgumannen

Ajkeslunda

Skär

Raukomr.

24,8

Bondans

Ajkesträsk

Ullahau

Avanäs

Norrsund

Kalbjärga

Fårö

Lauter

22,3

Skalasand

Lauterhorn

Vinor

Sudersand

Gamlahamn

Ringvida

Ava

Raukomr. S:t Olofs kyrka

St. Gåsmora

Sudersandviken

Båta

Avagrunn

Svingrunn

Mölnor

Aurgrunn

Fårö

Lansa

Ödehoburga

Verkegards

Limmorträsk

Fårösund

Dämba

Broa

Fårösund

Ryssnäs

Engelska kyrkogården

11,3

GOTLAND

Ryssudden

Dämba Misslauper

Bungeör

N

0 1 2 3 4 5 km

Regrettably the northernmost part of Gotland itself, and the adjacent Fårö, are within a military restricted area. This renders it difficult though not impossible for foreigners to visit Fårö. Foreign visitors may take a bus from Visby for a guided tour of the most interesting places on Fårö. And this is to be thoroughly recommended since Fårö is a singularly beautiful part of the Gotland islands – in the eyes of many people the most beautiful. There is a car ferry over Fårösund, 50 km north of Visby, to Broa on Fårö itself. The crossing takes about 15 minutes, but the ferry is liable to be crowded and there can be delays during the summer season.

It is popularly believed that this island derives its name from the many sheep that graze on the moorland (Får = Sheep, ö = island). This is not so however. The fact is the island was on the main route (farvägen) between East and West and it thus became known as Faar ö. Fårö is isolated in a way, yet it has always been visited by strangers, even though this may not have been their ultimate destination.

If Gotland itself is to some extent barren, Fårö is even moreso. Pines and junipers are twisted and stunted by a lifelong battle with the everlasting wind, while the rye struggles bravely in the meagre soil of the fields. Up here sea and shore have always been vital factors for man's survival and livelihood.

While life ashore on Fårö was harsh, life at sea was a constant adventure, the returns of which were seal or fish. The flotsam and jetsam along the shore could be a decisive element for the poor fisherman with his boat and plot of impoverished land. There has always been wreckage along Fårö's shoreline. There is an unwritten law that goods washed ashore belong to the people on that shore and the islanders' daily patrol along the beach was an essential feature of their existence. People up here have always been stubborn and individual, accustomed to managing their own affairs without interference from outsiders.

"A leaky boat and an obstinate female are the worse things on Earth" is a Fåröese adage. What could be worse than a leaking boat at sea or a nagging woman carping on about things to be done at home when the sealing ice has formed and the exciting and important adventure of the seal hunt is at hand?

Ärgerlicherweise ist der nördlichste Teil der großen Insel, ebenso wie die nördlich davon gelegene Insel Fårö, militärisches Schutzgebiet. Deshalb ist es schwierig, aber nicht unmöglich für Ausländer, Fårö zu besuchen. Man darf in Visby in einen Bus steigen und in Begleitung eines Fremdenführers die sehenswürdigen Plätze beschauen. Das läßt sich empfehlen, denn Fårö ist ein sehr hübscher Teil von Gotland, viele halten Fårö für den schönsten. Um hierher zu gelangen, muß man die Autofähre von Fårösund nehmen, ca. 50 km nördlich von Visby, nach Broa auf dem Fårö-Land. Die Überfahrt dauert ungefähr eine Viertelstunde, aber da Fårö vielleicht der bestbesuchte Teil der Insel ist während der Touristensaison, kann es doch eine Weile dauern, ehe man über den Sund kommt.

Viele meinen, die Insel sei nach den vielen Schafen benannt, die auf der Heide grasen, aber das stimmt nicht. Weil die Insel mitten in der Fahrrinne (farvägen) zwischen Ost und West lag, bekam sie den Namen Faar ö. In ihrer Art isoliert, und doch von Fremden besucht zu allen Zeiten, auch wenn sie sich vielleicht von Anfang an einen ganz anderen Bestimmungsort gedacht haben. Wenn die große Insel stellenweise karg ist, so ist Fårö es noch viel mehr. Kiefern und Wacholderbüsche sind verzerrt aufgrund ihres lebenslangen Kampfes mit dem ewigen Wind, und auf den mageren Feldern quält sich der Roggen tapfer. Hier sind Strand und Meer immer die Voraussetzung für die Existenz der Menschen gewesen, und gleichzeitig die Schatzkammer der Inselbewohner.

Wenn das Leben auf dem Lande dürftig war, so war es auf dem Meer ein Abenteuer, wo der Gewinn verteilt wurde in Form von Robben oder Fisch. Strandgut war vielleicht das, wovon ein armer Fischer, der ein Boot und ein Stückchen Acker besaß, überleben konnte, und Strandgut hat man immer auf Fårö gefunden. "Strandgut gehört dem Strandvolk", das war ein ungeschriebenes Gesetz, und genauso notwendig wie das tägliche Brot, waren die Touren am Meer entlang, um zu sehen, ob "Gott den Strand gesegnet hat." Das Volk hier draußen ist zu allen Zeiten stur und eigensinnig gewesen, daran gewöhnt, ohne Einmischung von Außenstehenden mit seinem Leben fertigzuwerden.

"Undichtes Boot und eigensinnige Alte sind die schlimmsten Dinge auf der Welt", lautet ein Sprichwort

The wild chive is a typical moorland bloom, spreading a lavender hue over the grey slopes.

Der wilde Schnittlauch ist die Blume des Heidebodens. Dann weicht das Grau einer violetten Wolke über dem grauen Erdboden.

There are sheep everywhere on Fårö, grazing contentedly on the moorland pasture.

Auf Fårö gibt es überall Schafe. Der magere Boden eignet sich gut für Schafweiden.

The English Cemetary is a pathetic memorial to the days of the Crimean War. A whole ship's crew, struck down by cholera, rest in this foreign field.

Der englische Friedhof ist ein Andenken aus den Tagen des Krimkrieges. Eine Schiffsbesatzung starb an Cholera und ruht an dieser fremden Küste.

71

The long stone walls are typical of Fårö — there is no shortage of building material!

Die langen Steinzäune sind typisch für die Insel. Das Material dazu liegt ja ganz in der Nähe.

There is a fine view of the sea from Fårö church. The modified exterior differs from that of the other Gotland churches.

Von Fårö Kirche hat man eine herrliche Aussicht über das Meer. Äußerlich unterscheidet sie sich von anderen gotländischen Kirchen.

The farm buildings are built of limestone, often thatched with *Cladium Mariscus* grass.

Die Höfe sind aus Kalkstein gebaut und die Wirtschaftsgebäude oft mit Dächern aus dem gezähnten Gras Cladium Mariscus versehen.

Following page
The Fårö coast has numerous facets. The rocky shores attract many fishermen.

Folgende Seite
Fårös Küste zeigt viele Gesichter. Die Klippenküsten locken viele Freizeitfischer.

Catching seal out here was a game of life and death. The frozen landscape of ice was anything but hospitable and your plight might become so desperate that you had to pour aquavit into your seaboots to keep your feet from freezing.

The coastline of Fårö is blessed in more ways than one; it is not only generous but also remarkably beautiful. Yet what else could the Good Lord have done when he discovered that the island's interior not only had rocks in the fields but also innumerable bogs and sour pine stands between those fields. He had no choice, of course, but to make the coastline bountiful and fair so that the people living here would have something to subsist upon and something to find pleasure in.

Both on Gotland itself and on Fårö there are monumental limestone pillars or "raukar". On Fårö the "raukar" are best found along the west coast between Digerhuvud and Lauterhorn. Like the giants of the sagas these appear as stone statues on the water's edge. They stand poised as though abruptly fossilized during a casual conversation, mouths open, gazing seaward with expressions of petrified astonishment. The "rauk" scenery attracts many visitors, unfortunately not all as appreciative of their surroundings as they should be. Certainly the idea of lighting a fire on the shore is tempting – but never, ever, against a "rauk". The heat can quickly crack and split the fragile limestone and ruin for ever one of nature's priceless monuments! Moreover, attempting to hack fossils out of these ageless pillars is not only an extremely foolish thing to do – it is strictly forbidden! Posterity must also inherit the right to behold the unique creations of nature. In summertime Fårö is the property of its visitors, this is not an exaggeration but the harsh truth. The first school groups arrive in early May, amateur biologists and birdwatchers even earlier. Then come the summer cottage people, holidaymakers and tourist buses, throughout the summer. But the Fårö islanders are hospitable souls who are quite prepared to make room for those who have but a brief vacation at their disposal.

The long sandy shore at Sudersand offers sun-warmed dunes and closeby is the Ulla Hau driftsand field. Desert-hot and white as driven snow the sand here undulates as though it had rolled in from the open sea – which is

auf der Insel. Was konnte schlimmer sein? Ein leckendes Boot auf dem Meer oder eine eigensinnige Frau, die über die Hausarbeit nörgelt, wenn das Robben-Eis kommt, denn Jagd war ein spannendes und wichtiges Abenteuer.

Das war ein Spiel mit dem Leben als Einsatz, den Seehund oder "kuten", wie man sie hier nennt, zu fangen. Die Eislandschaft war nicht sehr gastfreundlich, und manchmal mußte man Branntwein in die Stiefel gießen, damit die Füße nicht erfroren.

Die Küste von Fårö ist auf viele Art und Weise gesegnet. Sie ist nicht nur fruchtbar, sondern auch sagenhaft schön. Aber was sollte der liebe Gott wohl machen, als er merkte, daß das Innere der Insel nur Steine auf den Äckern abbekommen hatte und hier und da einige Sümpfe und dürftige Kiefernhänge. Natürlich mußte er dann zusehen, daß die Küste reich und hübsch wurde, damit die Menschen hier draußen etwas hätten, von dem sie leben und worüber sie sich freuen konnten.

Auf der großen Insel, aber ganz besonders auf Fårö, gibt es monumentale Steinsäulen, die man "Raukar" nennt. Auf Fårö findet man sie am leichtesten an der Westküste zwischen Digerhuvud und Lauterhorn. Den Riesen in den Sagen gleich, sind sie zu Steinsäulen an der Wasserkante geworden. Als ob sie gerade eben in einer gemütlichen Unterhaltung abgebrochen wurden, stehen sie da mit offenem Mund, auf das Meer hinausspähend, und mit dem Ausdruck ewiger Verwunderung in ihren erstarrten Gesichtern. Die Rauk-Landschaft lockt viele Besucher an: nicht alle zeigen die gleiche vor dem, was die Natur ihnen Ehrfurcht bietet. Sicher ist es verlockend, am Strand ein Feuer anzuzünden, aber niemals an einem Rauk! Der leicht zu beschädigende Kalkstein kann durch die Hitze zerspringen, und die Welt wird ein Ereignis ärmer. Aus den Kalksteinen Fossilien herauszubrechen, ist nicht nur unverzeihlich dumm, das ist außerdem streng verboten. Auch nachfolgende Naturfreunde sollen die Schönheit der Natur genießen können.

Im Sommer haben die Touristen Fårö in Besitz genommen – das ist keine Übertreibung, sondern kraße Wirklichkeit. Die ersten Schulklassen kommen Anfang Mai, die Feldbiologen und Vogelschauer noch früher. Dann folgen solche, die den Sommer über hier wohnen und dann Urlauber und Touristenbusse den ganzen Som-

precisely what it has done. It is a fascinating experience to wander across these dunes and anyone interested in insects can study at leisure here the sinister activities of the antlion which digs its traps for unsuspecting victims in the sand. Another, more unusual inhabitant is the long-horned beetle, *Ergates Faber*, occasionally to be found in dead pines.

Fårö is a true seafarers' island and the boat has always been the most important feature of the islanders' life. One encounters boats wherever one goes along these shores; newly tarred and well looked after, or old and at rest but cherished nevertheless. And the houses, too, are old and loved. Most of them are built in stone, the obvious building material throughout the Gotland islands, whitewashed with locally burned lime. There are also more modern houses of course, though these are not always as traditionally fitting as they might be. Fishing is still one of the most vital occupations on Fårö and there remain yet a few fishing settlements, the sheds and boathouses scrupulously cared for by their owners. One of the most exemplary of these is Helgumannen where perhaps once a holy man (Helg = Holy) gave comfort and reassurance to the fishermen before they put out to sea. At Lautersviken there is also the ruin of an ancient St. Olaf church.

Sheep on the roadways, wild strawberries under the juniper bushes, abandoned boats no longer carrying seafarers. An old-established culture can never be bought for money, but an appreciative individual may well be granted a small share in it.

mer lang. Aber die Einwohner von Fårö rücken großzügig beiseite für die, die nur einen kurzen Urlaub haben.

Der lange Sandstrand bei Sudersand bietet sonnenwarme Sanddünen an, ganz in der Nähe liegt das Flugsandfeld Ulla Hau. Heiß wie die Wüste und weiß wie schneebedeckte Gipfel liegt der feine Sand wellenförmig, als ob er vom Meer hergerollt sei; und das ist genau das, was er gemacht hat. Es ist herrlich, durch die Dünen zu wandern, und wer sich für Kleingetier interessiert, kann versuchen, die Ameisenlöwen näher zu studieren, die ihre Fanggruben im Sand haben. Ein eher ungewöhnlicher, aber nicht ganz seltener Gast ist der Ergates Faber, der Riesen-Holzbock, der sich auch in abgestorbenen Kiefern zurechtfindet.

Fårö ist wirklich eine Seefahrerinsel, und das Boot ist seit uralten Zeiten das Wichtigste im Leben der Insulaner gewesen. Überall entlang den Stränden findet man Boote, frischgeteert und wohlbehalten, alt und ausgedient, aber immer geliebt. Auch die Häuser sind alt und geliebt. Fast immer aus Stein gebaut, dem natürlichen Baumaterial auf ganz Gotland. Weißgetüncht mit dem Kalk, den man selbst brannte. Es gibt natürlich auch neuere Häuser, nicht alle der alten Tradition getreu. Einige Fischerdörfer gibt es auch noch, und die Schuppen werden von ihren Besitzern gehegt und gepflegt. Auch heute noch ist der Fischfang lebensnotwendig auf der Insel. Eines der hübschesten Fischerdörfer heißt Helgumannen (Heiliger Mann), vielleicht gab es da einmal einen Heiligen, der den Fischern Trost und Kraft versprach vor der Fahrt auf das Meer. Bei Lautersviken liegen auch die Reste der alten Olofskirche.

Lämmer auf den Wegen, Walderdbeeren unter den Wacholderbüschen, ausgediente Boote, die aufgehört haben, Seeleute zu tragen. Alte Kultur kann man nicht für Geld kaufen, aber ein bescheidener Geist kann vielleicht ein wenig daran beteiligt werden.

Following pages
The boat is an integral part of Fåröese life — well kept and newly tarred or an abandoned wreck, its place is nevertheless by the sea.

Folgende Seiten
Das Boot ist immer der Begleiter des Fåröbewohners. Fein und frischgeteert, oder alt und ausgedient, das Boot gehört auf den Strand, solange es lebt.

German version: Kerstin Johansson
English version: Alan Tapsell
Photographs: Key L Nilson
Maps: Erich Zenz
The maps have been cleared officially for publication.
Lantmäteriverket 1978-03-22
Layout: Per E Lindgren

Deutsche Übersetzung von Kerstin Johansson
Englische Übersetzung von Alan Tapsell
Fotos Key L. Nilson
Karten Erich Zenz
Die geographischen Darstellungen sind mit Genehmigung des Landver-
messungsamtes zur Veröffentlichung freigegeben. 22.3. 78
Graphische Gestaltung Per E. Lindgren

Andra utgåvan

AB Boktryck, Helsingborg 1993
ISBN 91-27-03503-4